The Drone Revolution:
Aerial Innovation and Its Implications

By

David E. Gee

TABLE OF CONTENTS

CHAPTER I
Introduction...**5**
    A. The Rise of Drones...5
    B. Importance of Aerial Innovation...8
CHAPTER II
Historical Perspectives on Aerial Innovation.......................................**12**
    A. Early Concepts of Aerial Vehicles.. 12
    B. Military Applications of Drones... 15
    C. Civilian Adoption of Drones.. 18
CHAPTER III
Technological Advancements in Drone Development........................... **23**
    A. Drone Hardware Evolution... 23
    B. Improvements in Battery Technology.. 27
    C. Civilian Adoption of Drones..30
CHAPTER IV
Drones in Various Industries...**35**
    A. Agriculture and Precision Farming.. 35
    B. Filmmaking and Entertainment...38
    C. Environmental Conservation and Research....................................42
    D. Infrastructure Inspection and Maintenance.................................... 45
CHAPTER V
Regulatory and Ethical Considerations...**49**
    A. Drone Regulations and Laws... 49
    B. Privacy and Security Concerns... 52
    C. Environmental Impact of Drone Usage... 56
CHAPTER VI
The Future of Aerial Innovation...**60**
    A. Advancements on the Horizon... 60
    B. Integration of Drones into Urban Spaces.. 64
    C. Artificial Intelligence and Swarm Technology................................. 67
CHAPTER VII
Socioeconomic Impact of Drones...**72**
    A. Job Displacement and Creation.. 72
    B. Economic Opportunities and Growth...75
    C. Global Perspectives on Aerial Innovation....................................... 79
CHAPTER VIII
Addressing Challenges and Limitations... **84**
    A. Safety and Risk Mitigation..84
    B. Public Perception and Acceptance..87
    C. Technological Limitations and Solutions... 91
CHAPTER IX

Drones and the Military..**96**
   A. Drone Warfare and Implications..96
   B. Ethics of Autonomous Drones...100
CHAPTER X
Aerial Innovation and Society...**105**
   A. Educational and Research Implications...................................105
   B. Accessibility and Inclusivity...109
   C. Art and Creativity in Drone Applications................................113
Conclusion..**118**
   A. Recap of Aerial Innovation's Journey.....................................118
   B. Reflection on the Broader Implications...................................122
   C. Prospects for the Drone Revolution's Future..........................126

CHAPTER I
Introduction

A. The Rise of Drones

In the not-so-distant past, the skies were the domain of birds and aircraft piloted by humans, but a remarkable technological shift has occurred in recent decades, ushering in the era of drones. The rise of these unmanned aerial vehicles (UAVs) has been nothing short of revolutionary, permeating various aspects of modern life and transforming industries in unimaginable ways.

Drones, initially developed for military applications, have rapidly expanded their reach to civilian and commercial domains, leading to an aerial innovation that has captured the world's attention. The driving force behind this meteoric rise lies in the convergence of several key factors, including advancements in miniaturization, battery technology, artificial intelligence, and the affordability of consumer electronics.

One of the primary catalysts for the drone revolution was their adoption by the military. Drones provided military forces with unprecedented reconnaissance capabilities, reducing the need to put human lives at risk in dangerous missions. These unmanned aircraft could conduct surveillance, gather intelligence, and even carry out targeted strikes with unparalleled precision. The military's success with drones sparked interest and investment in their further development.

As technological breakthroughs continued, drones started to penetrate the civilian and commercial markets. From aerial photography and filmmaking to agriculture and infrastructure inspections, drones found applications in numerous industries. They offered cost-effective and efficient solutions that were previously unattainable, opening up new possibilities for businesses and entrepreneurs alike.

Moreover, the widespread availability of consumer drones fueled the imaginations of hobbyists and enthusiasts. With a user-friendly interface and built-in safety features, recreational drones became popular among people of all ages, turning the skies into an accessible playground for millions.

The rise of drones, however, has not been without controversy. The use of armed drones in military operations has raised ethical questions about the consequences of remote warfare and the potential for civilian casualties. In the civilian sphere, concerns have been raised about privacy and security as drones equipped with cameras can intrude into private spaces or become tools for nefarious activities.

Despite the challenges and concerns, the drone revolution marches on, driven by innovation and creative applications. Researchers and engineers continue to push the boundaries of drone capabilities, with breakthroughs in artificial intelligence enabling autonomous flight and swarm technology that allows coordinated actions of multiple drones.

As we delve into the world of drones and aerial innovation, this book aims to explore the history, technology, applications, and implications of this transformative phenomenon. From examining the impact of drones on various industries to considering the regulatory and ethical challenges they pose, we will journey through the fascinating landscape of the drone revolution. This book seeks to provide an in-depth understanding of the current state of drones and offer insights into the future possibilities they hold for society and the world at large.

B. Importance of Aerial Innovation

The advent of aerial innovation, particularly in the form of drones, has brought about a wave of transformational changes that extend far beyond the confines of the aviation industry. The importance of this revolution lies in its potential to reshape the way we interact with technology, conduct business, and address societal challenges in the 21st century.

Aerial innovation has unlocked a vast array of possibilities, empowering industries to achieve feats that were once deemed impractical or cost-prohibitive. From agriculture to filmmaking, infrastructure inspection to environmental conservation, drones have proven to be versatile tools that enhance efficiency, data collection, and decision-making processes. For instance, in the field of precision agriculture, drones equipped with advanced sensors can monitor crops in real-time, allowing farmers to optimize irrigation, fertilization, and pest control. This not only increases crop yields and resource efficiency but also contributes to sustainable agricultural practices.

In the realm of filmmaking and entertainment, aerial shots that once required helicopters or cranes can now be captured with drones, offering filmmakers unprecedented creative perspectives. The use of drones in this context not only lowers production costs but also enhances storytelling, immersing audiences in awe-inspiring visuals that were previously unattainable.

Furthermore, drones have emerged as powerful tools for environmental conservation and research. They facilitate the monitoring of wildlife populations, habitat assessment, and the tracking of environmental changes, aiding scientists in their efforts to better understand and protect fragile ecosystems. This aerial perspective enables a comprehensive view of environmental issues, enabling targeted conservation efforts and informed policy decisions.

Aerial innovation has also played a crucial role in revolutionizing infrastructure inspection and maintenance. Traditional methods of inspecting bridges, power lines, and tall structures often required human inspectors to physically access hazardous or hard-to-reach locations. Drones, on the other hand, can navigate these areas with ease, capturing high-resolution imagery and identifying potential issues. This not only ensures the safety of workers but also reduces downtime and maintenance costs.

Beyond its practical applications, the significance of aerial innovation extends to its potential to bridge gaps in education, research, and humanitarian efforts. Drones can be valuable tools in educational settings, engaging students in hands-on learning experiences in science, technology, engineering, and mathematics (STEM) fields. Moreover, in remote or disaster-stricken areas, drones can be deployed for delivering medical supplies, conducting search and rescue operations, and providing vital aid and relief.

As with any technological advancement, the rise of drones also brings forth challenges that must be addressed to fully harness their potential. Privacy concerns, security risks, and the integration of drones into urban spaces are among the complex issues that demand attention.

In this book, we delve into the depths of aerial innovation, exploring its historical roots, technological advancements, diverse applications, and the ethical and regulatory implications it poses. By understanding the importance of this transformative phenomenon, we can better navigate the complexities of integrating drones into our society, unlocking their myriad benefits while ensuring responsible and sustainable use for the future.

CHAPTER II
Historical Perspectives on Aerial Innovation

A. Early Concepts of Aerial Vehicles

The desire to conquer the skies and achieve flight has captivated human imagination since ancient times. Early civilizations, inspired by the graceful flight of birds, sought to replicate this marvel through various ingenious inventions and concepts. The quest for aerial vehicles marks the embryonic stage of aerial innovation, laying the foundation for the astonishing advancements that would follow.

Among the earliest recorded attempts at aerial innovation are the mythological tales of Daedalus and Icarus in Greek mythology. According to the legend, Daedalus, an expert craftsman, constructed wings using feathers and wax for himself and his son Icarus to escape imprisonment on the island of Crete. While their flight was initially successful, Icarus, carried away by the thrill of soaring through the skies, flew too close to the sun, causing the wax to melt, and he tragically fell into the sea. Though this mythical account represents the human fascination with flight, it also serves as a cautionary tale about the risks and limitations of early aerial experiments.

Throughout history, inventors and innovators from diverse cultures have envisioned various contraptions that aimed to achieve flight. Chinese inventors during the Han Dynasty developed kites, which provided some insight into the principles of lift and airflow. In the Islamic Golden Age, polymath Abbas Ibn Firnas conducted one of the earliest recorded attempts at gliding flight in the 9th century, constructing a winged apparatus that allowed him to glide for a short distance.

In the 15th century, Leonardo da Vinci, the famed Italian polymath, sketched designs for numerous flying machines, including ornithopters with flapping wings, parachute-like devices, and aerial screws resembling modern-day helicopters. While da Vinci's inventions remained conceptual and were never built during his lifetime, his visionary ideas laid the groundwork for future aerial innovation.

The 18th and 19th centuries witnessed a surge in ballooning experiments, as inventors sought to harness the power of hot air and hydrogen to achieve controlled flight. In 1783, the Montgolfier brothers, Joseph-Michel and Jacques-Étienne, successfully demonstrated the first untethered hot air balloon flight in France. This event sparked a ballooning craze and furthered the understanding of atmospheric conditions and buoyancy.

While these early concepts and experiments were significant steps forward, it wasn't until the late 19th and early 20th centuries that powered flight became a reality. Pioneers like the Wright brothers, Orville, and Wilbur Wright, achieved the first powered, controlled, and sustained flight in 1903, fundamentally transforming the course of history and opening the skies to an era of unparalleled aerial innovation.

The early concepts of aerial vehicles may have been riddled with failures and setbacks, but they exemplify humanity's unwavering determination to conquer new frontiers. From mythological dreams to the visionary sketches of da Vinci, these early glimpses into aerial innovation laid the groundwork for the technological marvels that we enjoy today. As we explore the historical perspectives of aerial innovation, it becomes evident that each step in this journey has contributed to shaping the present landscape of drones and aerial technology.

B. Military Applications of Drones

Military applications have played a pivotal role in the development and evolution of aerial innovation, with drones emerging as a transformative force in modern warfare. The use of unmanned aerial vehicles (UAVs) in military operations traces its roots back to early experiments and concepts that sought to minimize the risks faced by human pilots and enhance military capabilities.

The concept of military drones can be traced back to the early 20th century, with some of the first notable developments occurring during World War I. Inventors and engineers explored the idea of using radio-controlled aircraft, known as "aerial target" or "aerial torpedo" drones, to carry out aerial attacks against enemy positions. However, the technology of that era was limited, and these early attempts did not achieve widespread success.

It was during World War II that significant advancements were made in the field of military drones. Both Axis and Allied forces experimented with various types of drones, including target drones for training anti-aircraft gunners and radio-controlled aircraft designed to carry explosives for offensive missions. One notable example was the German V-1 flying bomb, an early cruise missile designed to strike London and other cities in Europe. The V-1, while not fully autonomous, represented a significant leap forward in the development of unmanned aerial weaponry.

The post-World War II period saw a shift in military strategy, with the advent of the Cold War and the rise of the nuclear age. Drones, now equipped with more sophisticated technology, were used for reconnaissance and intelligence gathering in high-stakes surveillance missions. These early reconnaissance drones, like the

Lockheed U-2 and the Ryan AQM-34 Firebee, were essential in monitoring enemy activities and providing critical information to military commanders.

During the Vietnam War, drones played a significant role in combat as well. The Teledyne Ryan BQM-34 Firebee, originally developed for reconnaissance, was adapted for use as a target drone to simulate enemy aircraft in training scenarios. Additionally, drones were utilized for electronic warfare, carrying jamming equipment to disrupt enemy radar systems.

The 21st century witnessed a dramatic increase in the use of drones in military operations, particularly after the September 11, 2001, terrorist attacks in the United States. The U.S. military, in particular, spearheaded the development and deployment of armed drones, such as the General Atomics MQ-1 Predator and the MQ-9 Reaper. These drones revolutionized modern warfare by providing real-time intelligence and the ability to conduct precision strikes against high-value targets with reduced risks to human pilots.

The use of military drones, however, has been a subject of debate and controversy. While they offer undeniable advantages in terms of reduced risks to human lives and enhanced surveillance capabilities, the deployment of armed drones has raised ethical concerns about civilian casualties and the implications of remote warfare.

As we explore the historical perspectives on aerial innovation, it is evident that military applications have been instrumental in driving the development of drone technology. From early experimental concepts to modern, sophisticated UAVs, military drones have played a critical role in shaping the landscape of aerial innovation and expanding the possibilities of unmanned flight in both military and civilian domains.

C. Civilian Adoption of Drones

While the inception of aerial innovation can be largely attributed to military applications, the widespread adoption of drones by civilians has emerged as a groundbreaking and transformative aspect of modern society. The journey of drones from military tools to consumer gadgets has been marked by technological advancements, changing regulations, and a burgeoning interest in exploring the world from above.

The civilian adoption of drones traces its roots back to the latter half of the 20th century when remote-controlled model aircraft and helicopters became popular among hobbyists and enthusiasts. These early radio-controlled aircraft, often constructed from basic materials like balsa wood, served as precursors to the sophisticated drones we see today. Hobbyists delighted in piloting these aircraft, immersing themselves in the joy of flight without leaving the ground.

The real turning point for civilian drones, however, came with the advent of affordable and capable consumer electronics in the late 20th and early 21st centuries. Miniaturization, improved battery technology, and the integration of powerful sensors enabled the creation of small, agile, and user-friendly drones. The launch of the first commercially successful consumer drone, the Parrot

AR.Drone, in 2010, marked a milestone in the democratization of aerial innovation.

The rise of consumer drones was also fueled by advancements in camera technology, as drones equipped with high-definition cameras opened up entirely new possibilities for aerial photography and videography. Aerial shots that once required expensive helicopters or cranes could now be captured with ease, allowing amateur photographers and filmmakers to achieve breathtaking aerial perspectives.

As the technology became more accessible and consumer-friendly, drones rapidly gained popularity in a multitude of industries. Aerial photography and videography became staples in filmmaking, advertising, real estate, and social media content creation. Drones allowed content creators to add a dynamic and captivating element to their work, engaging audiences with stunning aerial imagery.

In addition to the creative industries, drones found practical applications in areas like surveying, mapping, and inspection. Surveyors and cartographers leveraged drones' ability to rapidly capture high-resolution images and generate accurate 3D maps. In construction and infrastructure development, drones became indispensable tools for inspecting tall structures, pipelines, and power lines, reducing the need for risky manual inspections.

The widespread adoption of consumer drones, however, presented challenges related to regulation and safety. Governments around the world grappled with establishing rules and guidelines to ensure responsible drone use and address concerns about privacy and airspace congestion. Licensing requirements, no-fly zones, and altitude restrictions were implemented to strike a balance between innovation and public safety.

As drones continue to evolve and become more integrated into daily life, new applications and use cases emerge regularly. From drone delivery services to monitoring wildlife populations and aiding in disaster relief, the potential for civilian drone adoption appears boundless.

The history of civilian drone adoption exemplifies how technological advancements and changing attitudes toward unmanned flight have transformed drones from niche gadgets to ubiquitous tools with vast applications. As we explore the historical perspectives on aerial innovation, it is evident that the civilian adoption of drones has reshaped industries, elevated creative expression, and brought the wonders of aerial exploration within the reach of countless individuals worldwide.

CHAPTER III
Technological Advancements in Drone Development

A. Drone Hardware Evolution

The evolution of drone hardware stands as a testament to human ingenuity and relentless pursuit of pushing the boundaries of aerial innovation. From rudimentary designs to cutting-edge engineering marvels, the journey of drone hardware showcases the transformative power of technology in reshaping unmanned aerial vehicles (UAVs) into the sophisticated and versatile machines we see today.

In the early days of drone development, the focus was on creating basic, remotely piloted aircraft capable of carrying out specific tasks. These early drones were often constructed from lightweight materials like wood or aluminum to ensure ease of flight. They were equipped with simple radio controls, enabling operators to maneuver the drone from the ground.

As the decades passed, advancements in materials science led to the development of stronger and lighter components, paving the way for more complex drone designs. The introduction of composite materials and carbon fiber revolutionized drone construction, allowing for sturdier yet lightweight frames that significantly improved flight performance and endurance.

One of the most significant technological breakthroughs in drone hardware was the integration of electric motors and lithium-polymer batteries. Electric propulsion systems replaced internal combustion engines, providing quieter operation and better control. Lithium-polymer batteries offered higher energy density, extending flight times and enabling drones to cover greater distances.

The miniaturization of electronics played a vital role in drone hardware evolution. Smaller, more powerful microcontrollers, gyroscopes, and accelerometers enabled improved stability and flight control. These advancements paved the way for stable flight characteristics, making drones accessible to a wider audience, including hobbyists and commercial users.

The introduction of Global Positioning System (GPS) technology marked a turning point in drone hardware development. GPS allowed drones to autonomously navigate and follow pre-programmed flight paths with high precision. This not only reduced the workload for operators but also opened up possibilities for more sophisticated applications, such as aerial surveying and 3D mapping.

Camera technology has been a game-changer in drone hardware evolution. Early drones were limited to low-quality onboard cameras or external mounting options. However, the integration of high-definition cameras and gimbals allowed drones to capture stable and professional-grade aerial photography and videography. Drones became powerful tools for filmmakers, content creators, and photographers, revolutionizing visual storytelling.

Advancements in wireless communication further improved drone capabilities. Real-time video streaming from drones to ground-based controllers became possible, offering operators live feedback during flight missions. Additionally, improved connectivity facilitated the integration of drones into the Internet of Things (IoT), allowing for seamless data transfer and communication between drones and other smart devices.

As drone hardware continued to advance, the emergence of obstacle avoidance systems and collision sensors enhanced the safety and reliability of drones. These technologies, based on visual, infrared, or LiDAR sensors, enabled drones to detect and avoid obstacles, reducing the risk of accidents during flight.

Today, the ongoing research and development in drone hardware encompass a wide range of cutting-edge technologies. From vertical take-off and landing (VTOL) capabilities to artificial intelligence-powered autonomous flight systems, the future of drone hardware holds promises of further advancements and innovative applications in various industries.

The evolution of drone hardware from basic flying machines to sophisticated, intelligent aerial platforms reflects a relentless pursuit of engineering excellence. As drones continue to redefine possibilities and push the boundaries of aerial innovation, the trajectory of technological advancements ensures that the future of drone hardware will be as awe-inspiring as its past.

B. Improvements in Battery Technology

Among the most crucial and revolutionary advancements in drone development lies the continuous improvement in battery technology. The quest for longer flight times and increased power-to-weight ratios has been a driving force in shaping the capabilities of modern drones, enabling them to undertake more extended, complex missions and meet the demands of various industries.

In the early days of drones, flight times were severely limited by the weight and capacity of the batteries available. Early drone flights often lasted mere minutes before requiring recharging or replacement batteries. This severely restricted the practical applications of drones and hindered their potential to be used in tasks that demanded extended flight durations.

However, over the years, advancements in battery technology have been nothing short of revolutionary. Lithium-polymer (LiPo) batteries emerged as a game-changer for drones due to their high energy density and lightweight characteristics. Compared to traditional nickel-cadmium (NiCd) and nickel-metal-hydride (NiMH) batteries, LiPo batteries offer significantly higher energy storage capabilities, allowing drones to remain airborne for longer periods.

The transition to LiPo batteries significantly extended drone flight times, enabling hobbyists, photographers, and commercial operators to capture breathtaking aerial footage and carry out more extensive surveying missions. What was once a novelty limited to a few minutes of flight time became a practical tool with flight durations that could span upwards of half an hour or more.

Battery technology also played a crucial role in enabling the rise of consumer drones. As drones became more accessible and affordable, consumer demand grew, prompting manufacturers to prioritize the development of more powerful and efficient battery solutions. This not only enhanced the flying experience for hobbyists but also unlocked new possibilities for commercial applications.

Beyond merely extending flight times, battery technology improvements have facilitated the development of more capable and sophisticated drones. As drones became equipped with more powerful motors, advanced camera systems, and additional sensors, the need for batteries that could handle the increased power demands became evident.

Moreover, advancements in battery charging technology have made drone operation more convenient and efficient. Rapid charging solutions and smart battery management systems have reduced downtime between flights, allowing operators to maximize the use of their drones and carry out time-sensitive tasks with minimal interruptions.

While the evolution of battery technology has been remarkable, it continues to be a focus of ongoing research and development. Scientists and engineers are working tirelessly to develop even more efficient, safer, and eco-friendly battery solutions. Innovations such as solid-state batteries and energy harvesting technologies hold promises of further enhancing drone capabilities and sustainability.

As drones find applications in critical sectors like aerial surveying, infrastructure inspection, and search and rescue missions, the advancements in battery technology play a pivotal role in elevating their utility and impact. With each stride forward in battery innovation, drones become more than just flying machines; they become powerful tools that empower industries, drive progress, and redefine the possibilities of aerial innovation.

C. Civilian Adoption of Drones

The widespread adoption of drones by civilians has been fueled by an array of technological advancements, making these unmanned aerial vehicles (UAVs) more accessible, user-friendly, and versatile. From hobbyists to professionals, the allure of drones lies in their ability to provide a unique aerial perspective and the countless possibilities they bring to various industries.

One of the critical factors contributing to the civilian adoption of drones is the continuous improvement in drone affordability. As technology matured and production processes became more efficient, the cost of drone components, including sensors, motors, and batteries, significantly decreased. This reduction in manufacturing costs, coupled with the growing demand for consumer drones, led to a broader range of affordable options for the general public.

Advancements in miniaturization have also played a vital role in expanding the civilian drone market. Smaller, more compact designs have made drones more portable and easier to carry, attracting adventure enthusiasts, travelers, and content creators who seek to capture stunning aerial shots on the go.

Furthermore, improvements in drone control systems have democratized aerial exploration. In the past, flying a drone required specialized piloting skills, which limited its appeal to a niche audience. However, modern drones are equipped with intuitive remote controls and user-friendly interfaces that even beginners can quickly grasp. Additionally, advancements in GPS technology enable drones to incorporate autonomous flight features, simplifying complex maneuvers and making drone operation more accessible to a broader audience.

The integration of high-definition cameras and stabilization gimbals in consumer drones has revolutionized aerial photography and videography. Now, even amateur photographers and videographers can capture professional-quality aerial shots and cinematic footage. The ability to produce compelling visuals from the sky has opened new creative possibilities for content creation, social media influencers, and filmmakers alike.

In the commercial sphere, technological advancements in drone hardware and software have led to the rise of specialized drones for various industries. Drones equipped with thermal imaging cameras find applications in search and rescue missions, firefighting, and wildlife monitoring. Aerial surveying and mapping drones enable faster and more accurate data collection for construction, agriculture, and environmental monitoring.

Moreover, developments in battery technology have extended flight times and reduced downtime between flights, allowing commercial operators to cover more ground and carry out longer missions.

To support the growing civilian drone market, regulations have adapted to balance safety with innovation. Governments worldwide have established rules for drone registration, pilot certification, and no-fly zones to ensure responsible and lawful drone use. The evolution of regulations continues to accommodate technological advancements while addressing privacy and airspace concerns.

As drone technology continues to evolve, the possibilities for civilian adoption are boundless. From delivering packages and aiding disaster response to revolutionizing urban transportation, the future of drones holds exciting prospects for reshaping our daily lives and industries.

In conclusion, technological advancements have been instrumental in propelling the civilian adoption of drones. The convergence of affordability, user-friendly features, improved cameras, and specialized applications has made drones accessible to hobbyists, businesses, and professionals alike. As drone technology continues to mature, its impact on society and the economy will undoubtedly expand, further solidifying drones' position as a transformative and indispensable tool in the modern world.

CHAPTER IV
Drones in Various Industries

A. Agriculture and Precision Farming

Drones have emerged as a game-changing technology in the field of agriculture, revolutionizing the way farmers manage their crops and optimize agricultural practices. Precision farming, enabled by the capabilities of drones, has elevated crop yields, reduced resource wastage, and opened up new possibilities for sustainable agriculture.

One of the key applications of drones in agriculture is crop monitoring. Equipped with advanced imaging sensors, drones can capture high-resolution aerial images of fields, providing farmers with a comprehensive view of their crops' health and growth. These images help identify early signs of pest infestations, diseases, or nutrient deficiencies, enabling timely intervention and targeted treatments. By detecting issues early on, farmers can take appropriate measures to mitigate crop losses and optimize yields.

Drones also play a crucial role in precision spraying and fertilization. Traditional agricultural spraying methods often involve blanket application of chemicals across entire fields, leading to unnecessary use of pesticides and fertilizers. With drones, farmers can implement precision spraying, where chemicals are applied only to specific areas that require treatment, minimizing waste and reducing environmental impact. This targeted approach not only reduces chemical usage but also ensures that crops receive the right amount of nutrients and protection, enhancing overall crop health and quality.

Agricultural drones equipped with multispectral and thermal sensors enable crop stress analysis. By capturing data in various wavelengths, these sensors can detect variations in plant health, stress levels, and water distribution across fields. This information aids in precise irrigation management, optimizing water usage, and avoiding overwatering or underwatering crops. Efficient irrigation not only conserves water resources but also contributes to sustainable agricultural practices.

The integration of global positioning systems (GPS) and drone technology has facilitated the creation of precise field maps. Drones can survey fields and generate accurate 3D maps, providing farmers with valuable insights into soil health, topography, and drainage patterns. Armed with this data, farmers can implement site-specific management strategies, tailoring planting and cultivation techniques to suit the unique characteristics of each field. This targeted approach maximizes productivity and minimizes inputs, promoting environmentally friendly and economically viable farming practices.

Beyond traditional agriculture, drones are also revolutionizing the field of precision viticulture in the wine industry. Aerial imaging and remote sensing enable vineyard owners to monitor vine health, identify stress points, and predict crop yields. By understanding the unique needs of each vine, winegrowers can optimize grape quality and quantity, resulting in premium wines.

The use of drones in agriculture continues to evolve with advancements in technology and data analysis. Artificial intelligence and machine learning algorithms are being integrated with drone-collected data to enable even more sophisticated decision-making and automation in farming practices.

The adoption of drones in agriculture signifies a shift towards more efficient, sustainable, and data-driven farming. As drone technology becomes more accessible and specialized, the benefits of precision farming extend beyond individual farms, contributing to global food security and the responsible stewardship of our agricultural resources.

B. Filmmaking and Entertainment

The introduction of drones into the world of filmmaking and entertainment has sparked a creative revolution, unlocking breathtaking possibilities for capturing awe-inspiring visuals and transforming storytelling on the big and small screens.

Drones equipped with high-definition cameras and stabilizing gimbals have become invaluable tools for filmmakers and videographers seeking to elevate their craft. These aerial platforms allow filmmakers to capture stunning, sweeping shots from vantage points that were once inaccessible or required expensive equipment like cranes or helicopters. Whether it's a majestic aerial panorama of a natural landscape or an exhilarating chase sequence, drones add a new dimension of visual storytelling that captivates audiences and immerses them in the cinematic experience.

In the realm of feature films and television, drones have enabled directors to achieve creative shots that were previously unattainable. Iconic scenes shot with drones have become emblematic of modern filmmaking, showcasing the unparalleled perspectives that aerial shots can provide. Directors can now choreograph elaborate action sequences or intimate emotional moments from above, adding a touch of grandeur and intimacy simultaneously.

In addition to traditional filmmaking, drones have become essential in the realm of advertising and marketing. From capturing eye-catching commercials to creating compelling social media content, drones help brands and content creators stand out in a crowded digital landscape. Aerial footage of products, events, or destinations lends a unique visual flair that grabs viewers' attention and enhances brand messaging.

Drones have also revolutionized the world of sports and live events coverage. In sports broadcasting, drones capture dynamic angles and provide viewers with a bird's-eye view of the action on the field. These shots offer a fresh and immersive perspective that enhances the spectator experience and adds to the excitement of the event.

The entertainment industry has embraced drones in music videos, concerts, and live performances. Drones equipped with LED lights have been choreographed to create mesmerizing light displays, adding an element of spectacle to concerts and performances.

Beyond traditional media, drones have found applications in the realm of virtual reality (VR) and augmented reality (AR). Aerial footage captured by drones can be stitched together to create fully immersive 360-degree experiences, allowing audiences to virtually explore breathtaking locations and environments.

With the evolution of drone technology, filmmaking and entertainment have entered a new era of creative possibilities. However, the adoption of drones in this industry comes with the responsibility of adhering to regulations and ensuring the safety of operators, crew, and the public. Filmmakers must be mindful of the potential risks and respect the privacy and airspace regulations to foster a positive relationship between drone technology and the entertainment industry.

In conclusion, drones have transformed filmmaking and entertainment, enabling creators to capture extraordinary visuals and push the boundaries of storytelling. From Hollywood blockbusters to social media content, drones have become indispensable tools for capturing cinematic magic and captivating audiences worldwide. As drone technology continues to evolve, the future of filmmaking and entertainment holds exciting prospects, promising even more innovative and immersive experiences for audiences to enjoy.

C. Environmental Conservation and Research

Drones have emerged as powerful allies in the field of environmental conservation and research, transforming the way scientists, conservationists, and researchers study and protect the natural world. These unmanned aerial vehicles (UAVs) offer a unique and versatile platform for gathering data, monitoring ecosystems, and addressing pressing environmental challenges.

One of the key applications of drones in environmental conservation is wildlife monitoring. Equipped with advanced cameras and sensors, drones can survey vast and challenging terrains, tracking the movement of endangered species and monitoring their populations. By obtaining aerial imagery, researchers can gain insights into animal behaviors, migratory patterns, and habitat use, which inform conservation efforts and the development of protected areas.

In the realm of marine conservation, drones play a crucial role in studying ocean ecosystems and marine life. Marine biologists and researchers deploy drones to assess the health of coral reefs, detect harmful algal blooms, and monitor marine mammal populations. Drones equipped with hydrophones can even record underwater sounds, shedding light on the acoustic environment of marine habitats.

Drones have also become invaluable tools in monitoring and combating environmental threats, such as illegal logging, poaching, and deforestation. By patrolling vast forests and remote areas, drones can help authorities detect and deter illegal activities, protecting precious biodiversity and natural resources.

The integration of thermal imaging sensors in drones enables the detection of heat signatures, which proves beneficial in locating animals during rescue and conservation operations. For instance, drones have been used to identify and track injured or stranded animals, facilitating timely intervention and providing vital support to wildlife rehabilitation efforts.

In environmental research, drones are used to collect data in hard-to-reach or hazardous locations. Drones can access remote areas, such as glaciers, volcanoes, and disaster zones, to gather critical data without putting human researchers at risk. This data aids in understanding the impacts of climate change, natural disasters, and other environmental phenomena, contributing to improved disaster management and conservation strategies.

The mapping capabilities of drones offer invaluable assistance in land and ecosystem management. Drones can create high-resolution maps of forest cover, wetlands, and other habitats, providing accurate baseline data for conservation planning and monitoring changes over time.

Moreover, drones can be equipped with air quality sensors to assess pollution levels in the atmosphere. This monitoring helps identify pollution sources and evaluate the effectiveness of pollution control measures.

As drone technology continues to advance, artificial intelligence and machine learning algorithms are being integrated with drone-collected data. This allows for automated analysis of large datasets, expediting research processes and enhancing the accuracy of environmental assessments.

The use of drones in environmental conservation and research exemplifies how technology can contribute positively to the protection and understanding of our planet. With drones as powerful tools in their arsenal, environmentalists and researchers can collaborate more effectively to safeguard ecosystems, protect biodiversity, and address the urgent environmental challenges of our time.

D. Infrastructure Inspection and Maintenance

Drones have revolutionized the way infrastructure inspection and maintenance tasks are carried out, offering a safer, more efficient, and cost-effective alternative to traditional methods. From bridges and power lines to pipelines and tall structures, drones are becoming indispensable tools for ensuring the integrity and longevity of critical infrastructure.

One of the primary advantages of using drones for infrastructure inspection is their ability to access hard-to-reach or hazardous areas. Drones can navigate intricate structures and confined spaces with ease, eliminating the need for manual inspections by human workers in potentially risky environments.

In the realm of bridges and highways, drones equipped with high-resolution cameras and thermal sensors can identify structural defects, such as cracks, corrosion, and deterioration. These inspections provide valuable data to engineers and maintenance teams, enabling them to prioritize repairs and maintenance efforts effectively.

For power lines and utility poles, drones play a vital role in aerial inspections. Drones can survey power transmission and distribution lines, identifying potential issues like damaged insulators, loose connections, or vegetation encroachment. Timely detection of such problems minimizes the risk of power outages and ensures the reliability of electricity supply.

In the oil and gas industry, drones are deployed for pipeline inspections. Equipped with advanced sensors, drones can detect leaks, corrosion, and ground subsidence, helping operators address maintenance needs promptly and prevent potential environmental hazards.

The application of drones in infrastructure inspection extends to the construction sector as well. During construction projects, drones can monitor progress, capture aerial images and videos of the site, and assess the adherence to engineering plans and safety protocols. This data aids in project management and quality control, reducing the likelihood of errors and delays.

The adoption of drones for infrastructure inspection and maintenance is further enhanced by the integration of artificial intelligence and machine learning algorithms. These technologies enable drones to analyze inspection data in real-time, identifying anomalies and potential issues automatically. This level of automation streamlines the inspection process, allowing engineers and maintenance teams to focus on making informed decisions and taking timely corrective actions.

In addition to reducing costs and enhancing safety, the use of drones in infrastructure inspection offers environmental benefits. By minimizing the need for manual inspections and the use of heavy machinery, drones contribute to reducing the carbon footprint associated with maintenance activities.

As the technology continues to advance, drones are expected to play an increasingly significant role in infrastructure monitoring and predictive maintenance. With the ability to cover large areas quickly and collect vast amounts of data, drones are transforming the way industries approach infrastructure integrity, ensuring safer, more resilient, and sustainable systems for the future.

CHAPTER V
Regulatory and Ethical Considerations

A. Drone Regulations and Laws

As the use of drones continues to proliferate in various industries and recreational activities, governments worldwide have recognized the need for comprehensive drone regulations and laws to ensure safe and responsible drone operations. The establishment of clear guidelines and restrictions aims to strike a balance between enabling innovation and safeguarding public safety and privacy.

Drone regulations typically encompass a wide range of aspects, including drone registration, pilot certification, operational limitations, and airspace restrictions. Many countries require drone owners to register their aircraft with civil aviation authorities, ensuring accountability and facilitating the identification of drone operators in case of accidents or misuse.

Pilot certification and licensing are essential components of drone regulations, especially for drones used in commercial activities. Commercial drone operators are often required to undergo training and obtain a certification that demonstrates their competence in piloting and adhering to safety protocols.

To ensure safe drone operations, authorities impose operational limitations such as altitude restrictions, distance from airports, and no-fly zones around sensitive areas like government buildings, hospitals, and critical infrastructure. These restrictions aim to prevent incidents that could endanger public safety or disrupt airspace operations.

In addition to physical limitations, drone regulations address ethical considerations related to privacy and data protection. Drones equipped with cameras raise concerns about potential invasions of privacy when used irresponsibly or without consent. Regulations often stipulate guidelines on where drones can and cannot record images or videos to safeguard individuals' privacy rights.

The enforcement of drone regulations is a significant challenge for authorities, given the increasing popularity of drones and the diverse nature of drone operations. To address this, some countries have established designated drone operation areas or "drone parks" where drone enthusiasts can fly their aircraft safely without conflicting with other airspace users or violating regulations.

While drone regulations are essential for safety and compliance, they must remain adaptable to accommodate technological advancements and evolving use cases. Authorities must regularly review and update regulations to keep pace with the rapidly changing drone landscape and address emerging challenges.

Public awareness and education are crucial components of responsible drone use. Many countries and organizations run campaigns to inform the public about drone regulations, safe flying practices, and the ethical considerations associated with drone usage. This proactive approach encourages drone operators to be responsible and respectful of others' rights and privacy.

In conclusion, drone regulations and laws play a vital role in shaping the responsible and ethical integration of drones into our daily lives. Striking the right balance between promoting innovation and addressing safety and privacy concerns is crucial to unlock the full potential of drones while fostering a positive and sustainable drone ecosystem for the future. As technology advances and drone applications continue to diversify, the need for well-crafted and adaptive regulations will remain paramount to ensure safe, beneficial, and socially responsible drone operations.

B. Privacy and Security Concerns

The rapid proliferation of drones has raised significant privacy and security concerns, prompting governments, organizations, and individuals to grapple with the delicate balance between technological innovation and protecting fundamental rights. As drones become more accessible and capable, addressing these concerns becomes essential to ensure responsible and ethical drone usage.

One of the primary privacy concerns related to drones is the potential for unauthorized surveillance and data collection. Drones equipped with high-resolution cameras can capture images and videos from vantage points previously unattainable, raising questions about the extent to which individuals' privacy may be invaded. People fear that drones could be used for intrusive purposes, such as spying on private property or capturing footage in areas where people have a reasonable expectation of privacy, like their backyards or through windows.

To address these concerns, many countries have implemented privacy regulations specific to drone usage. These regulations may include requirements for drone operators to inform individuals when recording is taking place or obtain consent in certain situations. No-fly zones around private properties, sensitive areas, and places of worship are often established to protect individuals' privacy and prevent unauthorized drone operations.

Data security is another significant concern regarding drones. Drones equipped with cameras and sensors can collect large amounts of data, including images, videos, and geographical information. Securing this data and preventing unauthorized access or data breaches is crucial, especially when drones are used in sensitive industries like infrastructure inspection, research, or law enforcement.

The risk of drone-related cyberattacks and hijacking is also a growing concern. As drones become more interconnected and integrated into the Internet of Things (IoT), they may become vulnerable to hacking or unauthorized control. Such scenarios raise issues of public safety, as malicious actors could potentially manipulate drones to cause harm or disrupt critical operations.

Moreover, drones themselves can be used as tools for criminal activities, such as smuggling contraband or engaging in unauthorized surveillance. These illicit uses underscore the need for robust regulatory frameworks and technologies that can detect and prevent drone-related criminal activities.

Addressing privacy and security concerns surrounding drones requires a multi-faceted approach involving collaboration among governments, drone manufacturers, and industry stakeholders. Regulatory bodies must continuously review and update existing laws to keep pace with technological advancements and evolving use cases.

Drone manufacturers are also responsible for implementing security measures to protect users' data and prevent unauthorized access to their products. This includes ensuring that drone firmware and software are regularly updated to address potential vulnerabilities.

Public education is crucial to raising awareness about privacy and security risks associated with drones. Drone operators should be aware of their legal obligations, including respecting no-fly zones and privacy regulations. Additionally, individuals should understand their rights and how to report any violations they encounter.

By proactively addressing privacy and security concerns, society can unlock the full potential of drone technology while safeguarding individuals' rights and public safety. Responsible drone usage, coupled with strong and adaptive regulations, can pave the way for a future where drones benefit humanity while upholding ethical standards and protecting privacy and security in a rapidly evolving technological landscape.

C. Environmental Impact of Drone Usage

As the utilization of drones becomes more prevalent across various industries, it is essential to consider the environmental impact of their widespread adoption. While drones offer numerous benefits, they also pose environmental challenges that need to be addressed to ensure sustainable drone operations.

One of the key environmental concerns associated with drone usage is energy consumption. Drones rely on battery power for their operation, and while advancements in battery technology have extended flight times, the overall energy efficiency of drones remains a consideration. The energy-intensive process of manufacturing and disposing of drone batteries can contribute to a carbon footprint. However, efforts are being made to develop more sustainable battery options and explore alternative power sources, such as solar panels, to mitigate the environmental impact of drone energy consumption.

Drones used in aerial photography, surveying, and monitoring also generate electronic waste (e-waste) when their components reach the end of their lifecycle. Responsible e-waste management is crucial to prevent hazardous materials from polluting the environment and to promote recycling and safe disposal practices.

Furthermore, the noise pollution generated by drone operations can disturb wildlife and natural habitats, especially in sensitive areas such as wildlife reserves and national parks. Reducing the noise emissions of drones and adopting flight patterns that minimize disruptions to wildlife are essential considerations for mitigating their environmental impact.

The use of drones in agriculture and pesticide application has raised concerns about chemical pollution. While precision spraying by drones can reduce overall pesticide use, it is essential to ensure that the chemicals used are environmentally friendly and pose minimal harm to non-target organisms and ecosystems.

The impact of drones on wildlife must also be considered, especially when drones are used for wildlife monitoring and research. Repeated drone flights in close proximity to wildlife can cause stress and behavioral disturbances, potentially affecting breeding and foraging patterns. Researchers and conservationists need to establish best practices to minimize the disturbance caused by drones during wildlife studies.

To address the environmental impact of drone usage, it is crucial for governments and regulatory bodies to incorporate environmental considerations into drone regulations. This may include setting standards for energy efficiency, promoting sustainable manufacturing practices, and incentivizing the use of environmentally friendly materials and technologies in drone production.

The drone industry itself must also take responsibility for its environmental impact by adopting eco-friendly practices, reducing waste generation, and promoting the recycling and refurbishment of drone components.

Education and awareness among drone operators are essential for promoting environmentally responsible practices. Encouraging drone users to follow flight guidelines, avoid sensitive areas, and practice responsible e-waste management can collectively contribute to minimizing the environmental footprint of drones.

As drone technology continues to evolve, prioritizing the environmental impact of drone usage is paramount to ensure that the benefits they bring do not come at the cost of the planet's well-being. By integrating environmental considerations into drone operations and regulatory frameworks, society can harness the potential of drones while fostering a sustainable and responsible approach to their usage for the betterment of the environment and humanity alike.

CHAPTER VI
The Future of Aerial Innovation

A. Advancements on the Horizon

The future of aerial innovation holds exciting prospects as technological advancements continue to push the boundaries of what drones can achieve. From advancements in drone hardware and artificial intelligence to the integration of drones into smart cities and urban transportation, the possibilities are vast and transformative.

One of the most anticipated advancements on the horizon is the development of autonomous drones. The integration of artificial intelligence and machine learning algorithms will enable drones to make decisions and perform complex tasks without human intervention. Autonomous drones have the potential to revolutionize industries such as delivery, surveillance, and infrastructure inspection, making these operations more efficient and cost-effective.

Drone swarms represent another groundbreaking development in aerial innovation. By coordinating the movements of multiple drones, swarms can perform tasks collaboratively, acting as a unified entity. Swarm technology can significantly enhance search and rescue missions, disaster response, and environmental monitoring, as well as enable innovative applications in entertainment, light shows, and public displays.

Improved battery technology remains a focus of research, with the goal of increasing drone flight times and payloads. Advancements in battery chemistry and energy storage solutions will enable drones to cover longer distances and carry heavier payloads, unlocking new possibilities for long-range missions and specialized applications.

In the realm of urban transportation, the concept of air taxis and passenger drones is gaining traction. Electric Vertical Take-Off and Landing (eVTOL) aircraft, capable of vertical flight like helicopters but with quieter and more sustainable electric propulsion, are being developed for urban mobility. These aerial vehicles could revolutionize urban transportation, easing traffic congestion and providing faster point-to-point travel.

The future also holds possibilities for drones to play a pivotal role in environmental conservation. From monitoring deforestation and wildlife populations to aiding in reforestation efforts, drones equipped with advanced sensors and AI algorithms can contribute significantly to protecting and restoring the natural world.

The integration of drones into smart cities is another avenue of exploration. Drones equipped with sensors and cameras can collect real-time data on traffic, air quality, and infrastructure conditions. This data can be used to optimize city operations, improve emergency response, and enhance overall urban planning and sustainability.

Safety and airspace management will remain critical areas of development. Advancements in detect-and-avoid systems, airspace coordination, and drone traffic management will be essential to ensure the safe integration of drones into our skies, where they will coexist with manned aircraft and other aerial vehicles.

As with any technological advancement, ethical and regulatory considerations will continue to be important. Ensuring privacy, addressing security concerns, and implementing responsible use guidelines will be crucial to harnessing the full potential of aerial innovation while maintaining societal trust.

In conclusion, the future of aerial innovation promises a remarkable transformation of industries and urban landscapes alike. Advancements in autonomy, battery technology, swarm capabilities, and integration into smart cities will elevate the role of drones in various sectors, making them invaluable tools for solving complex challenges and improving our daily lives. By embracing responsible development and adopting ethical practices, we can shape a future where aerial innovation contributes positively to our society, economy, and the sustainable stewardship of our planet.

B. Integration of Drones into Urban Spaces

The integration of drones into urban spaces is a transformative vision that holds immense potential to revolutionize how cities operate, providing solutions to challenges such as transportation, public services, and environmental sustainability. As technology continues to advance, the concept of smart cities with drone-powered solutions is moving closer to reality.

One of the most promising applications of drones in urban areas is the concept of urban air mobility (UAM). Electric Vertical Take-Off and Landing (eVTOL) aircraft, commonly known as flying taxis or air taxis, are being developed to offer efficient and congestion-free transportation options within cities. These eVTOLs can transport passengers quickly between rooftops or designated vertiports, significantly reducing travel times and alleviating traffic congestion on the ground.

Beyond passenger transport, drones can revolutionize last-mile delivery services in urban settings. Drones equipped with cargo compartments can efficiently transport goods from distribution centers to homes and businesses, bypassing traffic and reducing delivery times. This could transform the logistics industry and improve the efficiency of urban supply chains.

In smart cities, drones equipped with various sensors can contribute to data collection for real-time monitoring and decision-making. For instance, environmental monitoring drones can measure air quality, temperature, and pollution levels, enabling cities to assess and manage their environmental impact more effectively. Additionally, drones equipped with cameras and analytics software can be deployed for traffic management, parking enforcement, and surveillance, improving overall urban safety and security.

Drones can also play a vital role in emergency response and disaster management in urban areas. Rapid-deployment drones can survey disaster-stricken areas, assess damage, and assist in search and rescue operations, providing critical situational awareness to first responders and aiding in efficient disaster recovery efforts.

However, the integration of drones into urban spaces also presents challenges that must be addressed. Airspace management becomes more complex with the addition of aerial vehicles flying in low-altitude urban environments. Ensuring safe drone operations while preventing collisions with other drones, helicopters, or manned aircraft will require sophisticated traffic management systems and detect-and-avoid technologies.

Moreover, concerns about privacy and noise pollution must be considered when deploying drones in urban areas. Striking a balance between the benefits of drone technology and respecting individuals' rights to privacy and tranquility will be essential in gaining public acceptance of drone integration.

To make the integration of drones into urban spaces a reality, collaboration among city authorities, drone manufacturers, and the public is crucial. Robust regulations and guidelines must be established to govern drone operations in urban environments, ensuring responsible and safe use.

The future of aerial innovation in urban spaces promises a paradigm shift in how we interact with and experience cities. By leveraging drones' capabilities, cities can become smarter, more efficient, and environmentally sustainable, ultimately improving the quality of life for residents and visitors alike. As these technologies continue to mature, the vision of drone-integrated smart cities is poised to become an inspiring reality that shapes the urban landscape of tomorrow.

C. Artificial Intelligence and Swarm Technology

Artificial Intelligence (AI) and swarm technology are poised to be transformative forces in the future of aerial innovation. The integration of AI algorithms into drones and the coordination of drone swarms promise to unlock unprecedented capabilities, enabling a wide range of applications across industries.

AI-equipped drones have the potential to operate autonomously, making intelligent decisions and executing complex tasks without constant human intervention. These smart drones can navigate through challenging environments, adapt to changing conditions, and optimize their flight paths to achieve specific objectives. For instance, in search and rescue missions, AI-powered drones can assess disaster-stricken areas, detect survivors, and plan efficient routes for emergency responders.

In the field of precision agriculture, AI-enabled drones can revolutionize farming practices. By analyzing data collected from sensors and imaging devices, drones can identify crop health issues, monitor soil conditions, and even predict yield outcomes. AI algorithms process this data to provide farmers with actionable insights, enabling precise and efficient agricultural management strategies.

AI's role in aerial photography and videography is also significant. Drones with AI-powered cameras can intelligently track subjects, maintain focus, and stabilize footage, resulting in professional-quality visuals. This feature is valuable for filmmakers, content creators, and live event coverage, adding a level of automation and creativity that enhances storytelling.

Swarm technology represents another exciting advancement in aerial innovation. Drone swarms consist of multiple drones operating collaboratively as a cohesive unit. The coordination of drone swarms allows them to perform tasks collectively, accomplishing objectives that a single drone could not achieve alone.

In disaster response scenarios, swarm technology can optimize search and rescue efforts. Drone swarms can cover large areas quickly, surveying terrain and identifying survivors more efficiently than individual drones. They can also work together to form communication networks in areas with damaged infrastructure, enabling real-time information exchange among first responders.

The versatility of swarm technology extends to environmental monitoring. Swarm drones equipped with various sensors can collect data across vast regions, providing comprehensive insights into air quality, climate patterns, and wildlife behavior. This data can contribute to better environmental conservation strategies and disaster preparedness.

Moreover, drone swarms have the potential to revolutionize the entertainment industry. Synchronized drone light shows and aerial displays have already captivated audiences with their mesmerizing choreography and visual spectacles. As swarm technology evolves, the scale and complexity of these performances will continue to push creative boundaries.

However, as AI and swarm technology advance, ethical considerations must be at the forefront of their implementation. Ensuring data privacy, preventing malicious use of autonomous drones, and addressing potential job displacement are important factors that need to be addressed.

The future of aerial innovation lies in the seamless integration of AI and swarm technology into drone operations. By harnessing the power of intelligent automation and collaborative swarms, industries can achieve greater efficiency, cost-effectiveness, and productivity. As these technologies continue to mature, they will undoubtedly reshape how drones are deployed, paving the way for a new era of possibilities in aerial innovation.

CHAPTER VII
Socioeconomic Impact of Drones

A. Job Displacement and Creation

The widespread adoption of drones is poised to have a significant socioeconomic impact, leading to both job displacement and creation across various industries. While drones bring numerous benefits in terms of efficiency and productivity, they also present challenges as they introduce automation and alter traditional job landscapes.

One of the primary concerns surrounding drones is the potential for job displacement in certain sectors. For example, drones are transforming the logistics and delivery industry by offering faster and more cost-effective solutions for last-mile delivery. As drone delivery becomes more prevalent, it could lead to a reduction in demand for traditional delivery personnel, such as couriers and drivers.

Similarly, the use of drones in agriculture is revolutionizing crop monitoring and spraying operations.

With the ability to cover large areas efficiently, drones can replace some manual labor tasks that were once performed by farmworkers. While this automation increases productivity and reduces costs for farmers, it may lead to job displacement in certain agricultural roles.

However, it is essential to consider that while drones may displace some jobs, they also create new opportunities and industries. The drone industry itself has witnessed substantial growth, leading to job creation in areas like drone manufacturing, software development, and drone service providers. Skilled drone operators, data analysts, and technicians are in demand to manage, maintain, and interpret the vast amounts of data collected by drones.

Moreover, as drones enable new applications and capabilities, entirely new industries are emerging. The rise of aerial photography and videography has led to a demand for drone pilots with expertise in capturing stunning aerial visuals for various media and marketing purposes. Similarly, the use of drones in construction and infrastructure inspection has created a demand for skilled professionals who can analyze drone-captured data and provide valuable insights for project management and planning.

To mitigate the potential negative effects of job displacement, reskilling and upskilling initiatives become crucial. As drone technology evolves, traditional workers in impacted industries can undergo training to acquire the skills needed to work alongside or complement drones. For example, delivery personnel can transition to managing and maintaining drone fleets, while agricultural workers can specialize in data analysis and precision farming practices.

Government policies and workforce development programs can play a vital role in facilitating a smooth transition in the job market. By investing in education and training programs that focus on drone-related skills, governments can equip the workforce with the tools they need to thrive in a drone-enhanced economy.

In conclusion, the socioeconomic impact of drones is multifaceted, with both job displacement and creation as drones reshape various industries. While there may be concerns about certain jobs being automated, it is essential to recognize the potential for new job opportunities and industries driven by the growth of drone technology. By fostering a supportive ecosystem that includes reskilling initiatives and forward-thinking policies, society can harness the full potential of drones while ensuring a sustainable and inclusive workforce in the age of aerial innovation.

B. Economic Opportunities and Growth

The widespread adoption of drones is opening up a plethora of economic opportunities and driving substantial economic growth across various sectors. Drones' versatility, cost-effectiveness, and efficiency have sparked innovation and generated new avenues for businesses, contributing to positive socioeconomic outcomes.

One of the key economic opportunities presented by drones lies in the realm of industry efficiency. In sectors such as agriculture, drones are revolutionizing traditional farming practices by offering precision agriculture solutions. Drones equipped with sensors and imaging technology can assess crop health, monitor soil conditions, and optimize irrigation, leading to increased crop yields and reduced resource wastage. By maximizing agricultural productivity, drones contribute to food security and drive economic growth in the agricultural sector.

The logistics and delivery industry is experiencing a significant transformation due to drone adoption. Last-mile delivery, one of the most expensive and time-consuming aspects of logistics, is becoming more streamlined and cost-effective with the use of drones. Drone delivery services are not only reducing delivery times but also lowering operational costs for businesses, enhancing their competitiveness and contributing to overall economic growth.

Drone technology is also creating opportunities in the realm of infrastructure development and maintenance. Drones equipped with high-resolution cameras and LiDAR sensors can efficiently inspect bridges, buildings, and power lines, identifying structural issues and facilitating timely repairs. The proactive maintenance enabled by drones enhances infrastructure safety, minimizes downtime, and leads to cost savings, promoting economic development in the construction and engineering sectors.

In addition to improving efficiency, drones are also fostering innovation in various industries. The entertainment and media sectors, for instance, are exploring new creative possibilities with aerial cinematography and drone light shows. The unique perspectives captured by drones add value to film and television productions and create captivating visual experiences for audiences, driving economic growth in the entertainment industry.

The proliferation of drones has led to the emergence of specialized drone services and solutions providers. Companies offering drone services, including aerial photography, surveying, and inspection, have witnessed substantial growth. This has created employment opportunities for skilled drone pilots, technicians, and data analysts, contributing to job creation and boosting the overall economy.

Moreover, the drone manufacturing industry has experienced significant expansion. As demand for drones continues to rise, manufacturers are investing in research and development, leading to advancements in drone technology and capabilities. This, in turn, stimulates economic growth in the manufacturing sector and promotes innovation-driven economies.

The economic impact of drones extends to tourism and the hospitality industry as well. Drones are used to capture breathtaking aerial views of tourist destinations and resorts, attracting more visitors and enhancing the overall tourism experience. The promotion of tourism through drone-generated content stimulates economic growth in the hospitality and travel sectors.

While drones offer substantial economic opportunities, it is essential to address regulatory considerations to ensure responsible drone use and public safety. Effective drone regulations can foster a conducive environment for drone innovation while addressing privacy, security, and safety concerns.

In conclusion, the socioeconomic impact of drones is undeniably positive, driving economic growth and creating opportunities in various industries. By leveraging drone technology, businesses can enhance their efficiency, expand their offerings, and explore new avenues for growth. Embracing responsible and ethical drone use, combined with supportive regulatory frameworks, will continue to unlock the full economic potential of drones, leading to a more innovative, sustainable, and prosperous future.

C. Global Perspectives on Aerial Innovation

The impact of aerial innovation and the proliferation of drones are not limited to specific regions but resonate on a global scale, influencing societies, economies, and industries worldwide. From developed nations to emerging economies, the transformative potential of drones is being recognized and harnessed, leading to diverse perspectives on their socioeconomic impact.

In developed countries, drones have already become integral to various sectors. The United States, for example, has seen significant growth in the commercial drone industry, contributing to job creation and economic expansion. Drone applications in agriculture, logistics, infrastructure, and public safety have streamlined operations, boosting productivity and driving economic growth.

European countries have also embraced drone technology for a range of applications, including precision agriculture, environmental monitoring, and aerial surveying. The European Union is actively working on developing a harmonized regulatory framework to foster innovation while ensuring safety and privacy compliance. Drones' economic potential is viewed as a catalyst for sustainable development and increased competitiveness.

In Asia, countries like China and Japan have emerged as key players in the global drone market. China is a major drone manufacturer, producing a significant portion of the world's drones and supplying them to various industries worldwide. Japan, on the other hand, has been at the forefront of drone technology research, utilizing drones in agriculture, disaster response, and infrastructure inspections. The region's drone advancements are seen as an opportunity to drive economic growth and improve efficiency across diverse sectors.

Drones are also making an impact in developing economies, offering innovative solutions to address specific challenges. In Africa, drones have been utilized for humanitarian purposes, including delivering medical supplies to remote areas and aiding in wildlife conservation efforts. The accessibility and cost-effectiveness of drones make them valuable tools in regions where traditional infrastructure may be limited.

South American countries are also adopting drones for a range of applications, from monitoring illegal logging and deforestation in the Amazon rainforest to improving agricultural productivity. Drones' ability to collect data and reach remote areas supports environmental conservation and economic development initiatives.

Global perspectives on aerial innovation also highlight the need for international collaboration and standardization. As drones transcend national borders, the harmonization of regulations, airspace management, and data privacy becomes essential for safe and seamless drone operations on a global scale.

While drones hold immense promise, there are also challenges that transcend geographic boundaries. Addressing privacy concerns, ensuring cybersecurity, and promoting responsible drone use are issues that demand international cooperation and best practices to build trust and ensure a positive socioeconomic impact.

In conclusion, the global perspectives on aerial innovation underscore the transformative potential of drones and their impact on societies and economies worldwide. As nations and regions leverage drone technology to drive economic growth, improve public services, and address pressing challenges, collaboration and ethical considerations will play a vital role in unlocking the full potential of drones while fostering a sustainable and inclusive future for all.

CHAPTER VIII
Addressing Challenges and Limitations

A. Safety and Risk Mitigation

As drones become increasingly prevalent in various industries and activities, addressing safety concerns and implementing effective risk mitigation strategies is paramount to ensure responsible and secure drone operations. While drones offer numerous benefits, they also pose unique safety challenges that must be carefully managed to safeguard both the public and the technology itself.

One of the primary safety considerations in drone operations is the risk of collisions with other aircraft. As the airspace becomes more crowded with drones, manned aircraft, and other aerial vehicles, the potential for accidents and near-misses increases. To mitigate this risk, authorities are developing systems for managing drone traffic, similar to air traffic control for manned aircraft. Implementing mandatory registration for drones and pilot licensing for commercial operators enhances accountability and promotes adherence to safety guidelines.

Another safety concern revolves around drone technology itself. Ensuring the reliability and redundancy of critical components such as propellers, motors, and batteries is crucial to prevent in-flight failures. Regular maintenance, pre-flight checks, and adherence to manufacturer guidelines are essential in minimizing the risk of technical malfunctions.

Weather conditions also play a significant role in drone safety. Strong winds, rain, fog, or extreme temperatures can adversely affect drone stability and navigation, potentially leading to accidents. Drone operators must be aware of weather conditions and avoid flying in adverse weather whenever possible to minimize risks.

The proximity of drones to people and property requires strict adherence to safety protocols. Guidelines for safe distances from people and buildings, especially in densely populated areas, are essential to prevent accidents and protect privacy. Moreover, drones equipped with cameras should be used responsibly and with consideration for individuals' rights to privacy.

To enhance safety and risk mitigation, advancements in drone technology are being employed. For instance, detect-and-avoid systems use sensors and onboard algorithms to help drones detect obstacles and take evasive actions to avoid collisions. Additionally, geofencing technology can prevent drones from entering restricted areas, such as airports or sensitive government facilities, further reducing the risk of accidents.

Pilot training and education are crucial elements in ensuring safe drone operations. Well-trained drone pilots are more equipped to handle unexpected situations and are knowledgeable about regulations and best practices. Implementing educational programs for both recreational and commercial drone operators fosters a safety-oriented drone culture and enhances overall drone operation standards.

Standardization and international collaboration are instrumental in addressing safety challenges on a global scale. Developing consistent regulatory frameworks and safety standards enables seamless drone operations across borders and fosters public confidence in drone technology.

In conclusion, prioritizing safety and implementing effective risk mitigation strategies are vital as drones become more integrated into various aspects of society. By addressing safety concerns, investing in technology advancements, and fostering a culture of responsible drone operation, we can unlock the full potential of aerial innovation while ensuring the safety and well-being of individuals and communities worldwide.

B. Public Perception and Acceptance

As drones become a more common sight in the skies, addressing public perception and gaining widespread acceptance for drone technology is critical for their successful integration into society. While drones offer numerous benefits, public perception can be influenced by various factors, including privacy concerns, safety fears, and misconceptions about their applications.

One of the primary challenges in gaining public acceptance for drones is privacy. The presence of drones equipped with cameras raises concerns about potential intrusions into individuals' private lives. The fear of unauthorized surveillance or data collection by drones can lead to negative perceptions and resistance to their use. To overcome this challenge, transparency and clear guidelines on drone operations, especially regarding data collection and privacy protection, are essential. Educating the public about the responsible and ethical use of drones can also help build trust and acceptance.

Safety is another significant aspect that influences public perception of drones. Reports of drone-related accidents or near-misses with manned aircraft can instill fear and raise doubts about their safety. Addressing safety concerns through strict regulations, pilot training, and technological advancements in detect-and-avoid systems can help alleviate public apprehensions.

Misconceptions about drones and their applications can also shape public perception. Media portrayals of drones in military contexts or sensationalized stories of misuse can create negative associations. To counter these misconceptions, highlighting the positive contributions of drones in industries like agriculture, environmental conservation, disaster response, and public safety is crucial. Demonstrating the beneficial uses of drones in everyday life can help the public recognize their value and potential for good.

Engaging with communities and involving the public in discussions about drone operations can foster acceptance. Involvement in public consultations, feedback mechanisms, and local community outreach initiatives can provide opportunities for open dialogue and understanding between drone operators and the public. Listening to concerns, addressing queries, and incorporating public input into drone policies can help shape more inclusive and socially responsible drone operations.

Furthermore, education plays a pivotal role in shaping public perception. Promoting awareness about the regulations governing drone use, their safety features, and the societal benefits they offer can help dispel myths and increase public understanding. Integrating drone education into school curricula and conducting public awareness campaigns can help normalize drones as valuable tools that contribute positively to various industries and daily life.

Partnerships between drone manufacturers, regulators, and community stakeholders are instrumental in addressing public perception challenges. Collaborative efforts can focus on responsible marketing, emphasizing safety measures, and addressing public concerns proactively. Building a positive and accurate image of drones through responsible communication is essential for building public trust and acceptance.

In conclusion, addressing public perception and gaining acceptance for drones is a critical aspect of their successful integration into society. By prioritizing privacy protection, enhancing safety measures, dispelling misconceptions, and fostering public engagement and education, we can pave the way for a future where drones are embraced as valuable assets that contribute to progress, innovation, and the betterment of our communities.

C. Technological Limitations and Solutions

While drones have achieved remarkable advancements, they still face certain technological limitations that impact their capabilities and applications. Addressing these limitations through continuous research, development, and innovation is essential to unlock the full potential of drone technology.

One of the primary technological limitations of drones is their limited flight time. Most consumer-grade drones can typically fly for only 20 to 30 minutes before requiring recharging. For commercial applications that require extended flight durations, such as search and rescue missions or large-scale surveys, this limitation poses challenges. To overcome this constraint, researchers are exploring improved battery technologies, including longer-lasting batteries and alternative power sources like hydrogen fuel cells and solar energy. These advancements aim to extend flight times and increase the operational range of drones, making them more versatile and efficient.

Another technological challenge lies in the miniaturization of sensors and payloads. As drones become smaller and lighter, integrating high-quality sensors, cameras, and other payloads can be challenging due to size and weight constraints. Advancements in sensor technology and miniaturization techniques are being pursued to allow drones to carry more sophisticated and advanced payloads, improving their data collection and analytical capabilities.

Stability and reliability during adverse weather conditions present another technological limitation. Strong winds, rain, and temperature extremes can affect drone performance and safety. Researchers are developing sophisticated control systems and stability algorithms to enhance drones' ability to withstand harsh weather conditions and ensure safe flight operations.

Navigational precision is crucial for many drone applications, such as surveying, mapping, and inspection. However, GPS signals can be unreliable or inaccessible in certain environments, such as urban canyons or indoor spaces. To address this limitation, researchers are exploring alternative positioning systems, such as visual odometry and LiDAR-based mapping, to improve drones' navigational accuracy in challenging environments.

The issue of limited communication range is also a technological limitation for drones, especially in remote areas or beyond line-of-sight operations. Establishing robust communication links is vital for real-time data transmission, remote control, and situational awareness. Advancements in communication protocols and satellite-based communication systems can extend the operational range of drones and enable applications like long-range delivery and beyond visual line-of-sight operations.

Furthermore, autonomous decision-making is a key area for technological development. While drones can be pre-programmed for specific tasks, advanced autonomy is essential for more complex missions and dynamic environments. Integrating artificial intelligence and machine learning algorithms enables drones to process real-time data and make intelligent decisions, enhancing their adaptability and versatility.

As the drone industry grows, ensuring cybersecurity becomes a critical technological consideration. Drones are vulnerable to hacking and unauthorized access, which can lead to safety risks and data breaches. Implementing robust cybersecurity measures, such as encrypted communication and secure firmware updates, is crucial to safeguarding drone operations and protecting user data.

In conclusion, addressing technological limitations is integral to unlocking the full potential of drone technology and expanding their applications across industries. Ongoing research and innovation in battery technology, miniaturization, stability, navigation, communication, autonomy, and cybersecurity will pave the way for more capable, reliable, and secure drones. By addressing these challenges, the drone industry can continue to thrive and contribute to advancements in various fields, ultimately benefiting society as a whole.

CHAPTER IX
Drones and the Military

A. Drone Warfare and Implications

Drone warfare has emerged as a prominent feature of modern military operations, presenting both advantages and complex ethical implications. Unmanned Aerial Vehicles (UAVs), commonly known as drones, offer unique capabilities that have transformed the landscape of modern warfare.

One of the key advantages of drone warfare is the ability to conduct reconnaissance and intelligence gathering without putting military personnel in harm's way. Drones equipped with high-resolution cameras and advanced sensors can survey enemy territory, monitor movements, and provide real-time situational awareness to military commanders. This information is invaluable for strategic decision-making and enhancing the effectiveness of military operations.

Another crucial application of drones in warfare is targeted strikes against hostile elements. Armed drones, also known as Unmanned Combat Aerial Vehicles (UCAVs), can precisely deliver munitions to specific targets, eliminating the need for manned aircraft or ground troops in dangerous missions. The precision and reduced collateral damage associated with drone strikes are often cited as advantages of this approach.

Furthermore, drones offer extended endurance and loitering capabilities, enabling prolonged surveillance and waiting for the right moment to strike. This persistent presence over the battlefield provides continuous support to ground forces and enhances the military's ability to respond quickly to emerging threats.

However, drone warfare also raises ethical and legal concerns. The remote and detached nature of drone operations can reduce the psychological barriers to using force, potentially leading to a greater frequency of military engagements. The risk of desensitization to violence and the potential for unintended civilian casualties have sparked debates about the ethical implications of drone warfare.

The issue of sovereignty is another contentious aspect of drone operations. The use of armed drones for targeted strikes in sovereign territories raises questions about the violation of national sovereignty and the potential for diplomatic tensions. The legality of drone strikes conducted in areas where the host nation has not explicitly granted permission remains a subject of international debate.

The concept of "signature strikes" is another ethical concern. Signature strikes involve targeting individuals based on patterns of behavior or associations, rather than specific intelligence confirming their identities. Critics argue that such strikes raise questions of proportionality and the potential for targeting innocent individuals based on flawed intelligence.

Moreover, there are concerns about the lack of transparency and accountability in some drone operations. The use of drones by intelligence agencies for targeted killings without public disclosure or oversight has been criticized as undermining democratic principles and the rule of law.

Addressing these ethical implications requires robust oversight, transparency, and adherence to international humanitarian law. Establishing clear guidelines and protocols for drone operations, ensuring accurate intelligence, and minimizing the risk of civilian casualties are critical steps in maintaining the moral integrity of drone warfare.

In conclusion, drone warfare offers distinct advantages in intelligence gathering and targeted strikes, enhancing military capabilities and reducing risks to personnel. However, the ethical implications of drone operations, including civilian casualties and questions of sovereignty, warrant careful consideration and responsible governance. Striking a balance between leveraging drone technology for military effectiveness and upholding ethical standards is essential to ensure that drone warfare aligns with principles of humanity and respect for international law.

B. Ethics of Autonomous Drones

The development of autonomous drones, capable of making decisions and acting without direct human intervention, has brought forth a host of ethical considerations in military applications. The prospect of machines making life-and-death decisions on the battlefield raises complex moral questions that demand careful examination and international dialogue.

One of the primary ethical concerns surrounding autonomous drones is the issue of accountability and responsibility. With human operators removed from the decision-making loop, who bears responsibility for the actions of autonomous drones? Ensuring accountability for any potential errors or unintended consequences becomes challenging when human decision-makers are not directly involved in the drone's actions.

The principle of human agency is a critical aspect of ethical deliberations. Some argue that the use of autonomous drones raises questions about the attribution of moral responsibility for harm caused during military operations. Human decision-makers can be held accountable for their choices, but autonomous drones, acting based on algorithms and AI, lack the same capacity for moral reasoning and ethical judgment.

Moreover, the potential for unintended consequences is a significant ethical concern. Autonomous drones, while designed to follow predetermined rules and objectives, may encounter unforeseen situations on the battlefield. The risk of unintended harm to civilians or friendly forces raises questions about the moral implications of deploying machines with limited discernment capabilities.

Another ethical consideration is the dehumanization of warfare. With human operators removed from the immediate battlefield, the emotional and psychological distance between combatants and targets may widen. This dehumanization could have adverse effects on empathy and moral decision-making, potentially leading to a higher threshold for resorting to violence.

Transparency and explainability are vital ethical requirements for autonomous systems. Understanding the decision-making process of autonomous drones is essential for evaluating their actions and ensuring compliance with international law. The "black box" nature of AI algorithms can pose challenges in determining why a particular decision was made, making it difficult to assess the moral justifiability of autonomous drone actions.

The principle of proportionality, a fundamental tenet of just war theory, raises ethical concerns in the context of autonomous drones. Determining the appropriate level of force in a given situation requires complex judgment calls that may be beyond the capabilities of current AI systems. The risk of disproportionate responses to perceived threats underscores the need for human involvement in decision-making.

To address the ethical challenges of autonomous drones, several measures are necessary. International norms and regulations governing the development and use of autonomous weapons systems must be established through multilateral discussions and agreements. Clear guidelines on the permissible scope of autonomy and the roles of human operators are essential to ensure responsible deployment.

Developing AI systems that can explain their decisions, often referred to as explainable AI, is vital for ethical autonomous drones. Understanding the rationale behind a drone's actions enables better evaluation of its behavior and fosters greater public confidence in its ethical usage.

Public engagement and ethical debates involving diverse stakeholders are instrumental in shaping responsible drone policies. Involving experts, ethicists, military personnel, and civil society in discussions about the use of autonomous drones can yield comprehensive and balanced perspectives on this complex issue.

In conclusion, the ethics of autonomous drones in military applications raise profound questions about responsibility, accountability, human agency, and the dehumanization of warfare. Developing transparent and accountable autonomous systems, defining clear ethical guidelines, and engaging in international dialogue are essential steps toward addressing the ethical challenges and ensuring that autonomous drones align with fundamental principles of morality, international law, and humanity.

CHAPTER X
Aerial Innovation and Society

A. Educational and Research Implications

The rapid advancements in aerial innovation, driven by drone technology and related fields, have profound implications for education and research, reshaping how knowledge is acquired, disseminated, and applied in society.

In the realm of education, aerial innovation presents exciting opportunities to enhance learning experiences. Integrating drone technology into educational curricula offers hands-on and immersive learning opportunities for students of all ages. From elementary schools to universities, drones can be used to teach various subjects, including science, technology, engineering, and mathematics (STEM) disciplines.

In science classes, drones can serve as tools for environmental data collection, enabling students to study ecosystems, climate patterns, and biodiversity. In physics lessons, students can explore the principles of flight and aerodynamics by building and piloting drones. Furthermore, drones can be employed in history and geography classes to examine landscapes and historical sites from unique aerial perspectives, enriching students' understanding of the world.

For universities and research institutions, aerial innovation opens up new avenues for exploration and data gathering. Drones equipped with specialized sensors and imaging technology facilitate research in fields such as environmental science, geology, archaeology, and urban planning. Drones provide researchers with cost-effective and efficient means to access hard-to-reach areas and gather data that was previously unattainable.

Moreover, drone technology encourages interdisciplinary research collaborations. Experts from diverse fields, including engineering, computer science, biology, and social sciences, can collaborate on drone-related projects to address complex societal challenges. This multidisciplinary approach fosters innovation and holistic problem-solving.

Aerial innovation also encourages research and development in drone technology itself. Ongoing research into battery technology, materials science, artificial intelligence, and automation directly benefits the drone industry and accelerates technological progress. Academic institutions and research centers play a critical role in advancing drone capabilities, leading to improved safety, efficiency, and versatility.

In addition to formal education and research, aerial innovation also impacts informal learning and citizen science initiatives. Hobbyist drone enthusiasts and citizen scientists are contributing to various research endeavors, such as wildlife monitoring, environmental conservation, and disaster response. Citizen science projects involving drones empower individuals to actively participate in research and contribute to valuable data collection efforts.

As aerial innovation continues to evolve, there is a growing demand for skilled professionals with expertise in drone technology and related fields. Educational institutions are responding to this demand by offering specialized programs and courses in drone piloting, drone engineering, data analysis, and drone policy and regulations. These educational pathways equip students with the knowledge and skills required to navigate the emerging drone industry and address real-world challenges.

However, while embracing the educational and research potential of aerial innovation, ethical considerations must be emphasized. Teaching responsible drone use, privacy protection, and adherence to regulations is vital to instill a sense of ethical responsibility in drone operators and researchers.

In conclusion, aerial innovation has far-reaching implications for education and research, transforming the learning experience and expanding the frontiers of knowledge. Integrating drone technology into educational curricula empowers students with practical skills and fosters a deeper understanding of various subjects. For researchers, drones offer unprecedented access to data and enable interdisciplinary collaborations to tackle complex issues. Embracing the educational and research opportunities of aerial innovation while upholding ethical principles is essential for building a society that harnesses the full potential of drone technology for the greater good.

B. Accessibility and Inclusivity

Aerial innovation has the potential to revolutionize society by promoting accessibility and inclusivity across various domains. Drones and related technologies are breaking barriers and creating opportunities that benefit individuals from diverse backgrounds and abilities.

In the realm of accessibility, drones play a crucial role in reaching remote and underserved communities. In regions with limited infrastructure or challenging terrains, drones serve as vital tools for delivering medical supplies, vaccines, and emergency aid. By providing faster and more efficient access to essential resources, drones contribute to improving healthcare outcomes and saving lives in hard-to-reach areas.

In disaster response scenarios, drones offer unparalleled advantages in assessing damage and identifying areas of need. After natural disasters or humanitarian crises, drones equipped with cameras and sensors can rapidly survey affected regions, providing real-time data to aid response teams and prioritize rescue efforts. This enhances the efficiency and effectiveness of relief operations, ensuring timely assistance to those in distress.

Additionally, aerial innovation fosters inclusivity in industries like agriculture. Drones equipped with precision sensors and imaging technology enable farmers to monitor crops and soil conditions with greater accuracy. This data-driven approach to farming promotes sustainable agricultural practices, improves yields, and empowers small-scale farmers with valuable insights to make informed decisions.

In the realm of education, drones are becoming powerful tools for promoting inclusivity. The hands-on and engaging nature of drone technology appeals to students with diverse learning styles and abilities.

Additionally, drones can aid students with disabilities, providing new perspectives and learning opportunities in subjects like science, geography, and photography.

Furthermore, drones have proven beneficial in supporting individuals with disabilities. For those with mobility challenges, drones equipped with smart features like autonomous navigation and obstacle avoidance can serve as personal assistants, helping with tasks like fetching items or conducting simple surveillance.

The drone industry's efforts to promote accessibility extend to assistive technology development. Researchers are exploring ways to integrate drones with assistive devices to aid individuals with limited mobility. For instance, a drone equipped with a robotic arm can assist someone with a disability in performing tasks that would otherwise be challenging.

To ensure the broadest possible impact, it is crucial to address the digital divide. The cost of drones and the availability of necessary infrastructure can present barriers to accessibility, particularly in low-income regions. Governments and organizations are working to bridge this gap by supporting drone technology initiatives in underserved areas and providing training and resources to local communities.

Embracing inclusivity also means addressing environmental considerations. The impact of drone technology on ecosystems and wildlife must be carefully managed to ensure that the benefits do not come at the expense of environmental conservation. Striking a balance between innovation and environmental responsibility is vital for the sustainable integration of aerial innovation into society.

In conclusion, aerial innovation is a powerful enabler of accessibility and inclusivity, touching various aspects of society from healthcare and disaster response to education and assistive technology. By leveraging the potential of drones and related technologies, we can address societal challenges, empower marginalized communities, and create a more inclusive and equitable future. Emphasizing responsible and ethical drone use, investing in education and training, and promoting collaboration between stakeholders are key steps in harnessing the transformative potential of aerial innovation for the betterment of all individuals and communities.

C. Art and Creativity in Drone Applications

Aerial innovation has transcended conventional boundaries and emerged as a canvas for artistic expression, sparking new frontiers in the world of art and creativity. Drones have become powerful tools that artists and creative minds are harnessing to produce breathtaking visual experiences and challenge traditional artistic norms.

Aerial photography and videography are perhaps the most widely recognized artistic applications of drones. The unique vantage points that drones offer open up new perspectives for photographers and filmmakers, enabling them to capture awe-inspiring aerial views that were once impossible or costly to achieve. The fusion of artistry and technology allows artists to present landscapes, architecture, and events in ways that evoke wonder and imagination.

Drone light shows have also emerged as mesmerizing spectacles that redefine the possibilities of artistic performance. Synchronized fleets of drones adorned with LEDs create intricate patterns and dynamic displays across the night sky. These aerial performances have found their way into large-scale events, celebrations, and artistic presentations, captivating audiences with their visual brilliance and choreography.

In the world of fine arts, some artists are exploring drones as interactive installations and kinetic sculptures. Drones equipped with artistic elements, such as paintbrushes or light projectors, can create dynamic artworks on canvases or buildings in real-time. This fusion of technology and artistic expression challenges the boundaries of traditional art forms, offering an innovative and immersive experience for art enthusiasts.

Furthermore, aerial art has found its way into the field of environmental art and land art. Drones enable artists to create large-scale installations in remote or challenging terrains, often incorporating natural elements into their works. These aerial sculptures and installations blend art, nature, and technology, encouraging contemplation and reflection on our relationship with the environment.

Drones are also revolutionizing the art of storytelling. Filmmakers and content creators are using drone technology to enhance the visual narratives of their projects, adding dynamic and captivating aerial shots that heighten the emotional impact of their stories. The aerial perspective adds depth and scale to storytelling, amplifying the emotions and messages conveyed through the medium of film.

The integration of virtual reality (VR) and drones is yet another realm of artistic exploration. By combining VR technology with drones, artists can transport viewers into immersive aerial experiences, allowing them to virtually soar through landscapes and cityscapes, creating a sense of presence and connection with the environment.

As drone technology continues to evolve, the boundaries of art and creativity in drone applications are constantly being pushed. With advancements in AI and automation, there is potential for drones to become co-creators with artists, generating unique patterns and performances based on algorithmic creativity.

However, like all artistic expressions, the use of drones in art raises ethical considerations. Artists and creators must be mindful of privacy concerns and the impact of their work on the communities and environments in which they operate. Responsible and ethical drone use in artistic endeavors is essential to ensure that the boundary-pushing potential of aerial innovation aligns with principles of respect and social responsibility.

In conclusion, aerial innovation is revolutionizing the world of art and creativity, offering artists and creators new tools and perspectives to produce captivating and boundary-pushing works. The integration of drones in various art forms, from photography and filmmaking to performance art and installations, is redefining artistic expression and captivating audiences with immersive experiences. As the boundaries of aerial art continue to expand, responsible and ethical artistic practices will be integral to ensuring that the aerial canvas remains a source of wonder, inspiration, and positive impact on society.

Conclusion

A. Recap of Aerial Innovation's Journey

The journey of aerial innovation has been a remarkable voyage of human ingenuity and technological progress. From humble beginnings to a diverse array of applications, drones and related technologies have transformed industries, enriched lives, and opened new frontiers in creativity and exploration.

The history of aerial innovation dates back to the early concepts of aerial vehicles, from ancient legends of flying machines to Leonardo da Vinci's visionary sketches of flying contraptions. However, it was in the early 20th century that significant strides were made in the development of practical aircraft, paving the way for the drone technology we know today.

The military's early adoption of drones during World War I laid the foundation for their role in reconnaissance and surveillance. Subsequent decades saw the expansion of military applications, culminating in the use of armed drones in modern warfare. The military's embrace of drone technology has sparked ethical debates about drone warfare and autonomous drones, urging society to confront questions of responsibility and accountability.

In the civilian sphere, drones have revolutionized various industries. In agriculture, drones have become essential tools for precision farming and crop monitoring, contributing to increased efficiency and sustainable practices. In filmmaking and entertainment, aerial cinematography has elevated storytelling to new heights, offering breathtaking perspectives and enhancing the visual narrative.

The environmental and conservation sectors have leveraged drones to monitor ecosystems, combat wildlife poaching, and assess environmental changes. Aerial innovation has enabled researchers to access remote and challenging terrains, advancing scientific exploration and discovery.

Moreover, drones have played pivotal roles in disaster response and humanitarian efforts. Their agility and ability to access hard-to-reach areas have been instrumental in delivering aid, conducting search and rescue operations, and providing critical information during emergencies.

Beyond practical applications, drones have entered the realm of art and creativity, becoming instruments of artistic expression and immersive experiences. From aerial photography to drone light shows, artists and creators have pushed the boundaries of aerial art, captivating audiences with visually stunning and thought-provoking works.

Throughout this journey, the integration of artificial intelligence and automation has fueled the continuous growth of aerial innovation. AI-driven capabilities, such as autonomous navigation and decision-making, have expanded the potential of drones, enhancing their safety, efficiency, and versatility.

As we reflect on the journey of aerial innovation, it becomes evident that the possibilities for the future are boundless. The integration of drones into urban spaces, the development of swarm technology, and the expansion of AI-driven applications will shape the next chapter of aerial innovation.

However, with innovation comes responsibility. Addressing challenges such as safety, privacy, and ethical implications is essential to ensure that aerial innovation aligns with societal values and contributes positively to our communities.

In conclusion, aerial innovation has evolved from a mere dream to a reality that permeates diverse aspects of society. The journey has been one of exploration, transformation, and creativity. Embracing the potential of aerial innovation while upholding ethical considerations will allow us to navigate the future skies responsibly and reap the full benefits of this remarkable technological revolution. As we move forward, collaboration, education, and a commitment to using aerial innovation for the greater good will ensure that drones continue to enhance lives, advance knowledge, and inspire generations to come.

B. Reflection on the Broader Implications

As we reach the conclusion of the journey through aerial innovation and its multifaceted impact on society, it is essential to reflect on the broader implications of this technological revolution. The far-reaching consequences of drones and related technologies extend beyond specific industries, calling for thoughtful consideration of the opportunities and challenges that lie ahead.

One of the most significant implications of aerial innovation is the transformation of our understanding of the world. Drones have opened up new perspectives on our planet, providing captivating aerial views that foster appreciation for the beauty and complexity of the environment. These insights into our world can foster environmental consciousness, urging us to preserve and protect the natural resources that sustain life.

Moreover, aerial innovation has redefined how we interact with technology. Drones have become accessible tools for people of all ages and backgrounds, bridging the gap between technology and everyday life. The fusion of art, science, and creativity in drone applications has made technology more approachable, sparking interest in STEM fields and inspiring the next generation of innovators.

In the context of industry, aerial innovation has disrupted traditional practices and paved the way for greater efficiency and productivity. From precision agriculture to infrastructure inspection, drones have streamlined operations and reduced costs, allowing businesses to thrive in a rapidly evolving world.

The democratization of aerial capabilities has also had social implications, empowering communities with tools to address their unique challenges. In humanitarian efforts, drones have played pivotal roles in delivering aid, monitoring environmental disasters, and supporting refugee populations. By bridging geographical barriers and increasing accessibility, aerial innovation contributes to a more connected and compassionate global community.

However, the growing ubiquity of drones also raises concerns about privacy and security. Striking a balance between the benefits of aerial technology and the need to safeguard personal privacy is crucial. Responsible regulations and guidelines must be in place to protect individuals from potential misuse of drones and data collection.

The ethical implications of drone warfare and autonomous drones demand ongoing dialogue and international cooperation. Establishing norms and standards for the responsible use of military drones is essential to prevent unintended consequences and ensure adherence to international humanitarian law.

As we navigate the future of aerial innovation, addressing societal challenges and harnessing the potential for positive impact requires collaboration among governments, industry leaders, researchers, and communities. Together, we must cultivate an environment that fosters innovation while upholding ethical considerations and social responsibility.

Educational initiatives that promote drone literacy and responsible use are vital for nurturing a drone-savvy society. Emphasizing the importance of safety, privacy, and ethical guidelines will ensure that the benefits of aerial innovation are accessible to all, while minimizing potential risks.

In conclusion, aerial innovation has reshaped our world in profound ways, touching various aspects of society from art and education to industry and disaster response. As we embark on the next phase of this journey, it is essential to recognize the broader implications and embrace the opportunities while remaining mindful of the challenges. By fostering a culture of responsible innovation, collaboration, and ethical decision-making, we can harness the transformative potential of aerial innovation to create a brighter, more inclusive, and sustainable future for all.

C. Prospects for the Drone Revolution's Future

The drone revolution has come a long way, and the future promises even more profound transformations as the technology continues to evolve. The prospects for the drone revolution's future are boundless, with emerging advancements and applications that will shape various industries and societies worldwide.

One of the most exciting prospects lies in the integration of drones into urban spaces. Urban air mobility (UAM) is gaining traction, with companies exploring the possibility of using drones for passenger transportation and logistics within cities. UAM could revolutionize commuting, reduce traffic congestion, and improve emergency response times, ushering in a new era of urban transportation.

Moreover, the development of autonomous drones and swarm technology will redefine the capabilities of aerial systems. Autonomous drones can undertake complex missions without human intervention, opening up possibilities for applications such as package delivery, environmental monitoring, and infrastructure inspection with unprecedented efficiency and precision. Swarm technology, where multiple drones collaborate seamlessly, holds great potential for disaster response, search and rescue operations, and large-scale environmental assessments.

The drone industry is also poised to witness advancements in energy solutions. Improvements in battery technology and alternative power sources will extend drone flight times, enhancing their endurance and enabling longer-range missions. This progress will bolster the viability of drone applications in various sectors, from agriculture and construction to surveillance and wildlife conservation.

As artificial intelligence and machine learning continue to advance, drones will become smarter and more intuitive. AI-driven drones will possess enhanced situational awareness, decision-making capabilities, and adaptive behavior, making them safer and more reliable for complex tasks.

Furthermore, miniaturization and nanotechnology will lead to the development of even smaller and more agile drones. Micro-drones and insect-sized robots could revolutionize search and rescue operations in disaster scenarios and enable surveillance in environments that were previously inaccessible.

In the realm of data processing and analytics, advances in edge computing and cloud-based technologies will enable real-time data transmission and analysis. Drones will be capable of processing vast amounts of data in flight, making them invaluable tools for time-critical applications like disaster response and public safety.

While the future of the drone revolution holds great promise, it also demands responsible governance and ethical considerations. Regulation and policy frameworks must keep pace with technological advancements to address safety, privacy, and security concerns effectively. Balancing innovation with accountability will be vital in ensuring that drones contribute positively to society.

In conclusion, the prospects for the drone revolution's future are bright and full of potential. From urban air mobility and autonomous drones to advancements in energy solutions and AI-driven capabilities, the technological landscape of aerial innovation is evolving rapidly. Embracing responsible innovation, collaboration, and ethical decision-making will shape the future of drones as transformative tools that enrich lives, drive progress, and address societal challenges. The drone revolution is not only a technological revolution but also a social and cultural evolution that will shape how we interact with the world, each other, and the sky above us. As we navigate this exciting path, embracing the possibilities while upholding our values will pave the way for a future where aerial innovation positively impacts every aspect of our lives.